IØ161ØØ8

Published By
Temple of Inner Peace™

P. O. Box 3247
Negril, Jamaica, West Indies

First Edition

Temple of Inner Peace™

is a registered trademark of
Theo Chambers, Sharon Chambers
Malcolm X. Chambers & Amina Diop
Library of Congress Cataloging Publishing Data

ISBN 978-0977971640

UBUNTU

This Book Is Dedicated To The Memory Of
My Mother Victoria (Connie) Chambers
My Father Harold T. Chambers Sr
My Son Theo Chambers III

To My Wife & Best Friend
Sharon Oshun Parris Chambers

To My Daughters
Veronica Chambers, Shelly Worrell, Amina Diop

To My Son
Malcolm X. Chambers

To My Grandchildren
Juliet Chambers - Kiara Graham - Saniyah Chambers
-Keyshawn Chambers - Kamiah Chambers - Flora Clampet
Amin Williams & Gia Williams

To My Three Loving Sisters
Veronica Bisped - Amelia Hendricks & Alicia Dalien

To The Entire Human Race
and
Our Living Universe

NAMASTE

THEO*ism*
Basic Principles & Beliefs

1. *We Are Transient Visitors On Planet Earth*
2. *We Respect The Cosmic Laws of Creations*
3. *We Are Divinely & Uniquely Created*
4. *We Acknowledge And Respect The Human Tree Of Life, The Womb-Man*
5. *We Acknowledge The Doctor Within*
6. *We Acknowledge The Creator Within*
7. *We Acknowledge The One Universal Breath*
8. *We Acknowledge & Respect Mother Earth*
9. *We Acknowledge The Chaotic to Perfection and Perfection to Chaotic Universal Laws*
10. *We Acknowledge That We Are 100+ Trillion Cells Manifesting As Humans*
11. *We Feed Our Internal Universe a Cellular Nutrition Diet*
12. *We Acknowledge That We Are The Living Repository of Our Ancestors*
13. *We Acknowledge that Planet Earth is floating in Space in harmony with The Cosmic Laws.*
14. *We Acknowledge That Planet Earth Existed Before Humans and Can Do So Again*

Table of Content

FOREWORD

Life, a simple term that describes a very complex state of affairs and the ability to master one's existence, is the topic that the book "THEO*ism*" introduces.

A great friend, who happens to be a published author, Theo Chambers, penned his latest work to look in-depth at Life, Existence, Purpose, and how we can best be the Gatekeepers of our greatest gift from the Universe.

Writing a blueprint to share, this book gives an insightful, in-depth look at how individuals can assume a position that will serve as a steward to the Gift of Life that we are given.

Theo is a many faceted writer, prolifically and strategically touching on the delicate blueprint of creation.

His latest work focuses on how we are born with no previous assignment in life, only a transitory expiry date that to some degree of lifestyle choices, we can certainly commandeer!

Reading this work will help us to train and protect our bodies as the temples they were meant to be.

THEO*ism* is Chambers wake up call to the consciousness of the reader.

With his poignant, yet subtle style of writing, the THEO*ism* practitioner will evolve into an energy source that perpetuates an inquisitive mind.

This work will teach us to be conduits in our children's lives, not the mastermind of their plan.

Reading THEO*ism* will help one to understand that God, the Creator, gives us all the ability to perform at our maximum potential and perform miracles beyond explanation.

What is Success in Life, find out before your Transitory Earthly Vacation Passport expires...

Conimac McKithen, M.Ed
Promoter Music, Theater & Boxing

Are you enjoying your earthly experience
before your Transitory Vacation
Passport expires?

Introduction

Are you ready to explore the depths of your being as a creator? If you are, you will enjoy reading *THEOism*.

This book will challenge you to acknowledge and become the master of the universe within.

The premise of THEO*ism* as a lifestyle not dogma, allows truth to come to the surface, when one awakens to the awareness that consciousness is breathing you as part of the divine law.

"I AM because we are" (Ubuntu), takes on greater meaning. In this conscious awareness you and humanity are One and cannot be separated. Universal truth is immutable; we either live in harmony or disharmony, thus reaping the benefits of our actions.

Chambers guides readers to step outside the confines of the rational mind to see with clarity using the Socratic principle to establish truth in THEO*ism*, as he did in his first book God vs. Judaism & Christianity (2011).

Developing the art of questioning everything gives the seeker the tools to critically examine information which will form the basis of his knowledge and growth leading to spiritual development and self-mastery.

In *The Sage Within (2012)*, Chambers examines the inner power of the Sage to develop alchemical mastery and to manifest ones destiny through the varied experiences of

Goddess Farinah, the only female Sage in the fabled
Village of Watanama.

THEO*ism* offers the reader the opportunity to rise above
personal limitations and experience the world as a creator,
with limitless potentiality.

Twenty-first century thinking is challenged and advanced
by Chambers' unrelenting quest to push the envelope
of unconventional thinking to uncover the Cosmic Laws of
Nature which is our internal guide.

The enlightened being, living from the inside out,
effortlessly makes his mark on life by allowing his/her
Ancestors to come to life through the DNA.

Chambers, the visionary thinker, reveals the keys to
unlocking the universe within the pages of this seminal
book which should be in every home, school and public
libraries.

Sharon Parris-Chambers
Coach, Author, Speaker

• *Our Philosophy*

There is no absolute truth in our statements, conclusions, and theories because we leave the door open for discoveries that could influence our present ideologies. We approach all of our conversations fluidly, which allow us to adapt to new truth.
Theo Chambers

Theo is the Greek word for God. **THEOism** is a lifestyle that integrates the *Cosmic Laws of Nature* into its daily activities. We believe in the theory that we live 24/7 within our body; therefore, we are the master of *The Universe Within*.

THEO*ism* is not a religion. It does not have preachers, spiritual leaders, shamans, or ministers to teach.

THEO*ism* is a lifestyle whose principles are to live in harmony with nature by putting the *Planet Earth* (Gaia) first before our material desires.

THEO*ism* philosophy believes that within each living creature, including humans, exists the *Creative Force of Nature* (whom some call God).

We also accept the present truth that there are no known external forces that can define any one of us besides our internal world created by our own belief, ideology, philosophy, and understanding of creation.

THEO*ism* practitioners work tirelessly to execute our fiduciary duty to live in harmony with nature.

THEO*ism* is a series of conversations based on Socratic principles, which are a form of cooperative argumentative dialogs between individuals by asking and answering questions to stimulate critical thinking.

THEO*ism* has no beginning or end. Our conversations are focused on understanding *The Universe Within,* which in turn makes us better able to understand the external *Cosmic World.*

To successfully participate and benefit from the many **THEO*ism*** Conversations we will be having; you must temporarily put on hold your religious dogma, political philosophy, lifestyle, preferences, and all other beliefs.

You must enter the **THEO*ism*** *Temple of Inner Peace* with an open and analytical mind, *in search of truth*, and better understanding of *The Universe Within*.

THEO*ism* *conversations* are like an *Ancestry Wormhole* (essentially a shortcut through the universe).

It creates a shortcut for you to better understand yourself by allowing you to travel in time through your DNA to meet, speak with, and to understand the journeys of your Ancestors all who are *ALIVE* and living in your DNA.

• *My Journey*

I was about 12 to14 years old when my mentor, Professor Alfred Rowe (Now An Ancestor), took me to the beach around 6:00 a.m. one morning in Colon, Panama.

We sat on a big rock overlooking the ocean when he asked me to describe what I saw on the ocean floor.

I told him that I could see fish, stones, crabs, broken glass, and many other things.

We spent that morning discussing the philosophy of the Mystic Order of the Rose Cross, better known as the Rosicrucian.

I learned a lot that day when, surprisingly, around 1:00 p.m., he asked me again to describe what I was seeing.

I said that I could not give him a description of anything because the water was rough and muddy.

Professor Rowe then turned to me and said, "That Is Life.

One minute it's bright and sunny, and in a few hours, days, weeks or months, misery and chaos show its ugly face, but if you wait long enough, happiness and joy will return just like the ocean will become calm and crystal clear again."

I learnt that day that Joy and Misery are two sides of the same coin. Everything in life has its time and space to manifest, disappear, and reappear again.

To master life's changes, one must learn to dance with nature's changing rhythms without losing a beat.

THEO*ism* practitioners have adopted UBUNTU as one of their lifestyle principles.

• UBUNTU

I Am Because We Are is evidence through our DNA.

Our DNA is the repository of all of our Ancestors from all walks of life. *We Exist Because They Exist In Us!*

THEO*ism* practitioners accept as one of their truth that Ubuntu is The Spirit of Humanity… It's the awakening of our ancient past of living together in harmony which is one of the basic principles of **THEO*ism***.

"Ubuntu is the essence of being human. It speaks of the fact that my humanity is caught up and totally bound up in yours.

I am human because I belong. Ubuntu speaks about wholeness, it speaks about compassion.

A person with Ubuntu is welcoming, hospitable, warm, and generous, willing to share.

Such people are open and available to others.

They are willing to be vulnerable, they are affirming of others.

9

*They do not feel threatened that others are able and good,
for they have a proper self-assurance that comes from
knowing that they belong in a greater whole.*

*They know that they are diminished when others are
humiliated, diminished when others are oppressed,
diminished when others are treated as if they were less than
who they are.*

*The quality of Ubuntu gives people resilience, enabling
them to survive and emerge, still human despite all efforts
to dehumanize them"*

Reverend Desmond Tutu, *Nobel Peace Laureate*

UBUNTU

• *I Am Consciousness*

I will not let anyone walk through my mind
with their dirty feet
Mahatma Gandhi

The I Am Consciousness is that state of awareness and understanding which is like night and day between who you are as a person (Planetary Being) and who you become as a member of the human race (Worldly Being).

• Planetary Beings

THEO*ism* practitioners and coaches accepts the truth that for billions or even trillions of years, you and I existed in pure potentiality. By the intelligence of the *Cosmic Laws of Creation*, today, you and I are part of what we call the human race.

We are living in a planetary bubble and the *Ozone Layer* is our protective *Dome.* Everything we need to exist on planet earth exist under this *Dome.*

Everything outside of our *Planetary Dome* is detrimental to our existence. Therefore, it's our fiduciary duty to protect our Ozone Layer (Dome).

On *Planet Earth*, there are life forces essential to our existence, and we could suffer irreparable health damages or even death if we are cut off from oxygen for three minutes or more; three days without water, and three weeks without food.

Breathing uses chemical processes to send oxygen to every cell of our body and in the process, we breathe out carbon dioxide, the essential life energy of plants.

The carbon dioxide we breathe out is a result of the process of cell respiration, as is water.

During this process, energy is generated in the mitochondria of cells, and this energy is our physical life force, and this process cannot be completed without the presence of oxygen and glucose.

Glucose and oxygen interact together in cells to produce carbon dioxide and water, thus releasing energy. Once this process stops, the cells die.

Please note that the *Planetary and Spiritual Being* are one with nature and the universe.

THEO*ism* practitioners and coaches are conscious that the sole of our foot is part of a reflexology system with a brain of its own.

That is why our practitioners walk barefoot every chance they get because it stimulates those pressure points, especially when they walk on pebbles.

In future **THEO*ism*** conversations, we will be discussing and analyzing our WellBeing and how our worldly consciousness and actions get intertwined with our Planetary self.

This merger of two separate domains results in confusion as to who we are.

• Worldly Beings

THEO*ism* practitioners are fascinated by the process that transforms you and I from pure potentiality (a concept) into a worldly being.

Very few of us remember that we are *Planetary Beings* who were given an earthly transitory passport stamped with an expiration date.

Based on our worldly interactions, many of us end up leaving *Planet Earth* many years before our actual earthly transitory passport's expiration date.

Man's search for ways to live in harmony with nature and not become a victim of it has led to our creation, for example, of a place to live that will protect humans from the ravages of the weather system.

That was the embryonic birth of cave living that has now evolved into homes and mansions.

Our inability to travel a long distance in a short period led us to utilize horses and camels as means of transportation, which was the springboard for today's bicycles, motorcycles, jet planes, ships, automobiles, and virtual reality travel.

All animals and insects, including ants, have their own governmental and social hierarchical systems.

THEO*ism* practitioners and coaches were not surprised to learn that humans had also developed their ruling system with kings, queens, presidents, prime ministers, and chiefs.

We create Laws, and rules to give structure to our co-existence on *Planet Earth.*

The barter system came into existence, which led to our present monetary policies, including the newly emerging crypto and other virtual currencies.

Today, the size of our home and automobile model is a factor we use to determine someone's success status.

The designer branded clothes and accessories now play a significant part in the classification of our earthly class system called poor, middle class, upper class, and ultra-rich.

Our academic titles; doctor, lawyer, professor, nurse, engineer, carpenter, plumber, all those earthly academic accomplishments brand us in some human-made success boxes that have nothing to do with us as *PlanetaryBeings*.

Humans have developed sophisticated technology-driven businesses and a Social World to the point that has left us incapable of telling the difference between our *Planetary Responsibilities* and those of our *Earthly World LifeStyle*.

• Keep Both Domains Separate

THEO*ism* practitioners identify our human presence as an experience that applies to everyone regardless of his or her worldly success status.

Here are a few examples of *planetary encounters* that all humans go through equally.

THEO*ism* practitioners accept as the gospel truth that all humans were once attached to their mother's Umbilical Cord, and took approximately nine months to be born.

The joy, happiness, or sadness one feels at the birth of a child is the same feelings among all humans regardless of their social and economic status.

THEO*ism* practitioners acknowledge that if we remove the skin from all humans, our internal organs are the same.

We are a carbon copy of each other except for the amount of melanin in our bodies that determines our skin color.

Please note that babies, children, and blind people are *Racially Color Blind.*

Diseases affect all humans the same, and the death (transition) of loved ones, family, friends, associates, and even strangers trigger emotions in all human beings equally, regardless if they are poor, middle class, or super-rich.

The adrenaline that takes over our body when we got our first kiss is the same among all human beings regardless of our geographical location, money in the bank, family title, political affiliations, education, or religious dogma.

THEO*ism* practitioners and coaches see how man tries to overrule the *Creator's Laws of Nature* by using human-made ideology and belief for example;

The *Creator* of the cosmos made it possible for all males and females on *Planet Earth* to have a child with each other regardless of the color of their skin, economic or social success, still, humans say, whites should be with whites.

Blacks should be with blacks, and Jews should be with Jews.

Regardless of how hard humans try to overrule the *Cosmic Laws of Creation,* the basic rules of nature always prevail. This is grounded in the fact that when the sperm of a male comes face to face with the ovum of a female, it does not care one bit about economic or social accomplishments.

The only thing both of those cells are doing is singing the same song by Marvin Gay. *Let's Get It On.*

I guess my *Ancestor*s have revealed to all of us through my writings and their spiritual guidance how *Pure Energy and Vibration*, sometimes called *The Cosmic Laws of Nature* (God), will always win in the end.

When we are sleeping, rejuvenating our cells, and unconsciously communicating wirelessly with the *Creative Energy Force* that is responsible for our *Earthly Existence,* the process is the same for all of us whether we are sleeping in a twenty-million dollar home, or under a bridge.

Future **THEO*ism*** conversations will cover this point in more details.

Please be conscious of the truth; while sleeping, we have no influence.

It is when we wake up that, the world of chaos, racism, and confusion starts. That is when we remember that we are black, white, or Indian.

Once we are awake and conscious of our surroundings, that is when we mentally claim our chairman of the board status.

We remember that we have 10 million paper money or virtual currency in the bank. We are a member of X millionaire club. We are the inventor of XYZ product.

Some of us are brainwashed to believe that because our parents were born into a particular economic class, we cannot educate or earn our way out of that class system.

Please note that this has nothing to do with these individuals' planetary statuses and cosmic right to existence.

Some of us wake up with armed security guards at our doors and bulletproof automobile waiting to transport us because we are the political head of a country or chairman of a major corporation.

Our awakening conscious list of Worldly accomplishments is endless.

This awakened state reminds me of the metaphor by Swami Vivekananda that states:

Once there was a monkey, restless by its own nature, as all monkeys are.

As if that were not enough, someone made the monkey drink freely of wine, so that he became still more restless.

Then a scorpion stung him; it made him jump about for a whole day.

The poor monkey's condition became worse than ever. To complete his misery, a demon entered into him.

What language can describe the uncontrollable restlessness of that monkey?

The human mind is like that monkey; incessantly active by its own nature.
Then it becomes drunk by the wine of desire, thus increasing its turbulence.

Desire takes possession; there comes the sting of the scorpion of jealousy of others whose desires meet with greater fulfillment.

Last of all, the demon of pride takes possession of the mind, making it think itself of all importance.

How hard it is to control such a mind? It is our responsibility to control that restless, drunk, scorpion bitten, demon possessed mind, and to make it do certain things, attend to certain things, while refraining from doing other things and attending to distracting things

• *Human Creation*

"The word of God is the Creation we behold and it is this word, which no human invention can counterfeit or alter, that God speaketh universally to man."
Thomas Paine

The conversations we are about to have about human creation is not based on indisputable facts, but on what we presently understand to be truthful.

Therefore, each of our conversations leaves the door open to be proven wrong with future discoveries.

THEO*ism* accepts that our earthly creator is our mother's egg and father's sperm.

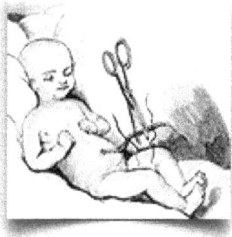

We are not disputing or challenging any religious belief that God is our creator.

We do not know of any other way humans are made but through the fusion of a mother's egg and father's sperm or *In-Vitro-Fertilization.*

If the above conversation is true, then it is safe to say that the building blocks of humans are cell based.

In the same breath, we can also state with absolute truth that our parent's egg and sperm are smaller than a grain of sand, and even though they are invisible to the naked human eyes, they possess all the blueprint and intelligence to create each one of us.

THEO*ism* practitioners believe that the creative intelligence (God) who empowered our parent's egg and sperm with the human creation blueprint, laid out the human creation process, and does not interfere with that process under any circumstance.

Women are the only carrier and manufacturers of ovum eggs and men of sperm. To date, there is no other means of creating human eggs and sperms.

Another truth is childbearing gives birth to the term: parents, mother, father, grandparents.

As you can see, **THEO*ism*** is a conversation each one of us should have with ourselves and the world around us in order to understand better;

- Who are we?
- Why are we here?
- From whence we came?

Where do we think we are going when nature automatically turns off our access to oxygen on the expiration date of our transitory earthly vacation passport?

Tracing, studying and understanding our *Ancestral* roots through our DNA, is the master key to unlocking the secret inside each of those potential moms (eggs) and Dads (sperms) living within us.

When we study the human creation process, it opens our third (3rd) eye to the truth that we live 24/7 within our body.

It is our godly obligation to keep our *Temple of Inner Peace* in optimum condition, and to keep our mind-body-soul in perfect synchronization with *The Universe Within* and the external *Laws of Nature*.

THEO*ism* conversations free us from any religious, political, and social ideologies by making us examine the raw facts that can be disputed or accepted, without invoking blind faith to accept a conclusion that cannot be proven truthful beyond a reasonable doubt.

To close this conversation, let us agree on one important point, **THEO*ism*** is an open conversation platform that can be used individually or in a group format.

The essential point about **THEO*ism*** is that it is non-judgmental. If you follow its conversations or not, it makes no judgment or tries to persuade you in any way, shape, or form.

You can leave each **THEO*ism*** conversation and pick up all your religious, political, and social lifestyle you placed on hold while participating in our discussions.

Your life will be back to normal unless you find **THEO*ism*** conversations so provocative that you plan to continue to participate in other discussions, or you find it so practical that you are willing to embrace its lifestyle.

• *Who We Are*?

With a curious zeal to better understand our own existence, we often go far out of our way to find out who we are and where we have come from. Why? We need to know, not just for the present, but from our earliest beginnings to the present.
Edward J. Fraughton

In our previous conversation entitled human creation, we spoke about the two intelligent cells that are responsible for our existence, which is our mother's egg and father's sperm.

THEO*ism* acknowledges that at birth, we come into this planet naked. We have no name, no title, no religious or political affiliation.

THEO*ism* believes that to date, no woman has ever given birth, and immediately after, a book of instructions comes out of her womb stating definitively who that child is, and what his or her role is going to be during that child transitory vacation on planet earth.

Before we complicate and confuse the identity of a newly born child, we need to ask, who is that child? From whence did he/she come?

What force was able to transform that child from pure potentiality into a living being?

Can you imagine that humans learn how to maintain their automobile in optimum condition?

They know when to get an auto tune-up, and they know what type of gas to add to their cars, such as premium, regular, or diesel.

We also learned what clothes are to be washed and those that need to go to the dry cleaners.

What we did not learn at home, school, or university, is who we are. What we need to eat and drink to keep our internal operating system in optimum performance.

Children today are learning to write complicated *Artificial Intelligence* codes, but those same children have no idea about the mapping code of the human body where they each live 24/7.

Ninety percent (90%) of humans have no idea how to optimize (feed) their immune system.

The Immune System is our defense against outside invaders that are trying to create chaos within our private sweet home where we all live 24/7.

THEO*ism* practitioners know that before we can repair or fix something, we need to understand how that item was built.

Based on that statement, humans cannot maintain a healthy internal defense force unless they truly understand the different functions of their inner world and what is needed to keep a cellular structure (human body) in perfect health. We acknowledge that there are about 100 trillion cells that make up the human body.

- We are not our names.
- We are not our titles.
- We are not our material possessions.

We are trillions of cells working in harmony expressing as you and I.

THEO*ism* believes that to become the master of our existence and the gatekeeper of our good health, we must understand how to read the human blueprint of creation.

We must learn from an early age that the genome of an organism is the whole of its hereditary information encoded in its DNA.

THEO*ism* conversations advocate for hospitals worldwide to be empowered with the facility to have the DNA tests done on every child that is born within 72 hours.

There should be a worldwide law that states that all adopted children have the indisputable right to have access to their adoption papers at the age of 21 and above.

THEO*ism* core conversations state that if we can accurately trace and identify our ancestors for thousands of years through our DNA, then those *Ancestors* are living within each one of us.

We are a living repository of our Ancestors, and our children and grandchildren for generations to come will be our repository when we transition into Ancestryhood.

We learn Kung Fu and Karate to protect ourselves against external aggression.

Before we can train our internal doctor (immune system), we need to acknowledge that cells are the tiny building blocks of life and that there are approximately 100 Trillion Cells in the human body.

Cellular Nutrition is the correct formula we need to keep our immune system optimized, and ready to defend our internal *WellBeing* against unwanted visitors?

Cellular nutrition puts the wisdom of the body to work by providing the cells with all the nutrients they need to operate at optimal levels.

If modern children are learning technology and programming at an early age, they can also learn that *Planet Earth* is approximately 4.5 billion years old and that human existence goes back about six million years.

Then they need to learn how humans survived for millions of years on *Earth* without a pharmaceutical industry that is only about two thousand years old.

UBUNTU

• *The Human Body*

*"The human body resonates at the same frequency as
Mother Earth.
So instead of only focusing on trying to save the earth,
which operates in congruence to our vibrations, I think it is
more important to be one with each other.
If you really want to remedy the earth, we have to mend
mankind. And to unite mankind, we heal the Earth. That is
the only way. Mother Earth will exist with or without us.
Yet if she is sick, it is because mankind is sick and
separated. And if our vibrations are bad, she reacts to it, as
do all living creatures."*
Suzy Kassem,

Followers of **THEO*ism*** share the belief that we should not confuse the great job that is being done by doctors and medical institutions, with the pharmaceutical industry.

The pharmaceutical industry is a financial profit-focused empire that uses doctors and medical institutions to push their products using skillfully crafted marketing and promotional strategies and medical financial incentives.

Having being a vegetarian for over 50 years, I did not realize that my body created extra cholesterol, resulted in me having a quadruple bypass in December of 2015 at the New York Veteran's hospital.

Out of all the medication I was prescribed, my holistic doctor told me to take the Metoprolol and the Atorvastatin Calcium. I went to mother nature, the rainforest, for all my additional medication.

Every morning my wife and I drink our natural juices. We eat lots of nuts, and we do our best to get our daily morning *Sunbath*.

The Sun, is *Planet Earth's* natural electrical grid, and without sunlight, all living things on *Earth* will eventually perish.

For thousands of years, man used nature's *Sunlight* to speed up the healing of wounds because it is a powerful non-toxic germ killer.

Can you imagine that our entire body is a sophisticated solar panel? And once we expose it to the Sun, it automatically starts to make vitamin D.

Please note that melanin is a natural *Sun-Blocker*. The darker your skin, the longer it takes your exposure to the Sun to produce vitamin D.

Sunbathing reduces blood pressure, it helps to improve blood circulation, eliminates toxins from the body, facilitates the bones in the absorption of calcium.

Sunbathing has a huge impact on mild depression.

Did you know that vitamin D produced by the sun's direct rays improves the function of your immune system by increasing the number of defensive white blood cells?

Vitamin D insufficiency affects almost 50% of the world's population.

Don't run from the Sun, welcome it. The Sun helps the doctor within to keep our body and the immune system optimized.

THEO*ism* conversations are deep-rooted in the theory that humans go to the rainforest for their medicine to combat *Earthly* related illnesses and many that are created by man's violation of *The Laws of Nature* and WellBeing.

What are some of those violations? We have violated *Nature's Laws on Clean Air*, *Clean Drinking Water*, and by creating artificial and laboratory-made food.

We feed our cells sugary drinks, and even today's bottled water has a PH level of less than 6.5, which means that they are acidic. Water should have a PH of 7.0 and above.

Deforestation is another human activity that causes the loss of trees and other vegetation.

Deforestation has a direct effect on climate change, flooding, soil erosion, fewer crops, greater greenhouse gases in the atmosphere that are causing the demise of indigenous people.

The rainforests make up 31% of the total landmass of the *Earth*.

Rainforests are vital in filtering carbon dioxide emissions from the air we breathe

Rainforests are also responsible for making oxygen which is essential for the survival of humans and wildlife.

We learned that half of the world's tropical forests had been cleared, and this has had a direct affect on biodiversity and the natural processes in the ecosystem.

Trees and all the fauna in the forests enrich the soil, and without the trees, the soil will lose its fertility, and the rise of bad agricultural practices causes soil degradation and erosion.

This erosion causes the soil to sweep into the rivers and ocean.

The forests absorb carbon dioxide and other greenhouse gas emissions, but due to deforestation,15% of these greenhouse gases are freed.

Deforestation is also contributing to the increase in temperature, climate change, and global warming.

THEO*ism's* Conversations acknowledges that trees play a vital role in the water cycle.

Trees keep the balance between the water on land and in the atmosphere. Deforestation disrupts the water cycle which has a direct effect on our weather conditions.

Today, we are building homes, hospitals, shopping malls, apartment buildings, restaurants, and even churches in the spaces that were once homes to insects, animals, medicinal plants, and many other microorganisms that are essential for a balanced ecosystem.

Now that we have invaded the living sanctuary of nature's insects we now call PESTS, we are doing our best to eliminate them by using chemicals and pesticides that are proven harmful to human health.

Insect (Pest) must be managed in a way that keeps them out of our homes while protecting both our homes, and the environment.

UBUNTU

• *Cannabinoid Receptors?*

"Some of my finest hours have been spent on my back veranda smoking hemp and observing as far as my eye can see."
Thomas Jefferson

THEO*ism* practitioners are fully aware of the seamless relationship between our internal world and the outer World we call *Planet Earth and the Cosmos*.

The following quotation is from Dr. Neil deGrasse Tyson (astrophysicist) when he was asked what is the greatest thing he admires about the universe?

Here is his answer:

"The most astounding fact is the knowledge that the atoms that comprise life on earth, that make up the human body are traceable to the crucibles that cooked light elements into heavy elements in their core under extreme temperatures and pressures.

These stars, the high mast ones among them went unstable in their later years, they collapsed and then exploded, scattering their enriched guts across the galaxy.

Guts made of carbon, nitrogen & oxygen and all the fundamental ingredients of life itself.

These ingredients become, part of gas clouds that condense, collapse to form the next generation of solar systems, stars with orbiting planets. Those stars now have the ingredients for life itself.

When I look up into the night sky and I know that we are part of this universe, we are in this universe; but perhaps more important than both of those facts is that the universe is in us.

When I reflect on that fact, I look up; many people feel small because the universe is big. I feel big because my atoms came from those stars."

Based on the above understanding of our cosmic connection, we are better able to understand why humans have an internal integrated cannabis tree called, cannabinoid receptors.

We are nature and nature is us!

THEO*ism* wellness conversations focuses on the fact that those who understand *The Universe Within*, are masters of their mind-body-soul synchronization and they possess the key to building a strong immune defense system.

One of **THEO*ism*** unwritten principles is based on the belief that the first person or group of individuals who received a doctorate degree, a nursing degree, a PHD or any other certification, got it from someone who did not have those credentials.

Based on the above truth, **THEO*ism*** acknowledges the existence of doctors, nurses, mathematicians, philosophers, scientists and geniuses long before the existence of modern colleges and university certification programs.

THEO*ism* practitioners are able to find quiet moments where the mind and nature become one, and during that process, we learn and acknowledge that the human body produces its own form of cannabis called the endocannabinoids system, which regulates circulation, mental function, and the immune and digestive systems.

THEO*ism's* first step during quietude, is accepting one of the few indisputable facts that we live and exist nowhere else but, inside of our bodies!

The Cannabis sativa plant, also known as marijuana, has been used for medical purposes throughout human history.

Around 5000 years ago, ancient China used extracts of the plant for relief of cramps and pain.

Our research revealed that the existence of cannabinoid receptors in the brain was discovered from in vitro studies in the 1980s.

We also learned that the *DNA sequence* that encodes a G-protein-coupled cannabinoid receptor in the human brain was identified and cloned in 1990.

Can you see how *The Universe Within* each one of us is a *Carbon Copy* of our external world?

Armed with such information, **THEO*ism*** practitioners are in constant pursuit of information, wisdom, and understanding about who truly exists within our bodies, and what can we do to keep it optimized, which in turn, allows us to enjoy our transitional vacation on planet earth with the least amount of internal chaos and illnesses.

That is why accessing *The Universe Within*, helps us to be able to decode the human internal blueprint of creation.

THEO*ism* practitioners understand that the cannabis plant is one of those human building block (fuel) components.

The *cannabis plant* contains chemical compounds that are unique to cannabis alone, and those compounds are called cannabinoids.

Cannabinoids interact naturally with special receptor sites on human cells called, cannabinoid receptors.

We have cannabinoid receptors because the human body creates naturally its own version of cannabis compounds called endocannabinoids which is the human body's THC.

Endocannabinoids connects into what has been termed the largest neurotransmitter networks in the human body called, neurotransmitter network that acts as a s*table regulator that helps maintain optimal balance in the body.*

It regulates circulation, mental function, and the immune and digestive systems.

THEO*ism* Conversations always emphasizes that an educated and informed **THEO*ism*** practitioners are empowered with the tools of life to be the masters of their WellBeing and Destiny.

Understanding CBD and its benefits is one of those tools necessary in order to regulate and control one's *Internal WellBeing*.

Cannabidiol (CBD), is the second most common of the active ingredients of marijuana. It is an extract from the hemp plant, which is a cousin of the marijuana family.

A *World Health Organization (WHO)* reports states that CBD exhibits no effects indicative of any abuse or dependence potential in humans.

Cannabidiol (CBD) is effective in treating some of the most sever childhood epilepsy syndromes by reducing the amount of seizures, and in some cases it was able to stop them altogether, which typically don't respond to anti-seizure medications.

THEO*ism* practitioners welcome the news that the FDA approved the first ever cannabis-derived medicine for these conditions, Epidiolex, which contains CBD.

Even though **THEO*ism*** practitioners believe that there is a big difference between a good night's sleep versus a good night's rest, we welcome the fact that CBD is commonly used to address anxiety, and for patients who suffer through insomnia, studies suggest that CBD may help with both falling asleep and staying asleep.

If we take our time to learn the various *Cosmic Laws of Communication*, we will be able to understand, like our *Ancestors* did, what nature is trying to tell us.

Example, A Jamaican pharmacologist professor by the name of Manley West, and an Ophthalmologist by the name of Albert Lockhart developed Canasol, The first Glaucoma Medical Marijuana Eye Drops in the Caribbean.

Professor Manley West

THEO*ism* practitioners continue to spread the true story of how Professor West listened carefully to country folks who told him that they were able to see better when they used an eye wash made up of ganja in water. Fishermen shared with professor West that when they drank ganja (*Tea*), their vision was a lot better.

Dr_Albert_Lockhart

Dr. Albert Lockhart discovered that his Rastafarian patients who used ganja had a low incidence of Glaucoma.

He noted that the eye drop, Canasol, upgrades the integrity of the optic nerve, the nerve which causes humans to see, thus, able to prevent blindness.

The Ganja plant quietly opened more of its hidden secrets by revealing to both Professor West and Dr. Lockhart, that its properties are also effective against motion sickness.

Back in the 1990s, Professor West developed Asmasol, another Ganja Infused Drug to treat Asthma, Colds and the Flu. It was effectively prescribed to children and adults.

What a wonderful *nature's medicinal plant Ganja* is!
Can you understand better why the pharmaceutical industry would do its best for medicinal Ganja not to see the light of day?

THEO*ism* practitioners *sarcastically always make this statement.*

It's a proven fact that the human body naturally produces its own cannabis called Endocannabinoids, and no government can pass a law prohibiting our internal energy from continuing to produce endocannabinoids (Cannabis).

Then, who gives government the power to declare a plant that is grown naturally on Planet Earth by the creator, to be labeled a drug and illegal to grow or use?

UBUNTU

• *Longevity Blue Zone*

"Let Food Be Thy Medicine, and Let Medicine Be Thy Food"
HIPPOCRATES

THEO*ism* practitioners travel the world physically and virtually in search of information on how people from around the world are living an active and disease free life up through their 90s.

On June 29, 2017, there was an article in oldwayspt.org entitled eating for Longevity: Lessons from centenarians.

Below is an excerpt from that article we are sharing with you so you can understand better how the *Cosmic Laws of Longevity* blessed those who respect its natural principles.

From the rugged mountains of Sardinia, Italy, to the sunny shores of Okinawa, Japan, traditional cultures around the world have a lot to teach us about good health and well-being.

Though "health through heritage" has been a guiding mission at Oldways for the past 27 years, geographers and anthropologists have renewed fervor over this concept by spotlighting places the world's longest-lived people call home.

These "Blue Zones," located between Asia, Europe, Latin America, and North America, maybe far apart both geographically and culturally, but they share significant similarities that play a central role in Longevity: lifestyle and diet.

The eating pattern of communities within the blue zones have not been influenced by Western diets.

They all follow the same basic principles: locally produced whole foods, plentiful vegetables and legumes, and high plant-based diets.

These regions hold the highest numbers of centenarians, and people living beyond the age of 100.

The majority remain physically active and disease-free into their 90s and beyond.

Okinawans have adopted the Chinese concept that food is "nuchi gusu,i," meaning "medicine for life," with properties that can help to prevent and treat illnesses and maintain health.

Essential eating habits include high consumption of local vegetables, soybeans, seaweed, sweet potatoes, and turmeric, and a low intake of salt.

Mediterranean diet, consisting largely of vegetables, healthy oils, whole grains, fruits, and legumes, with meat reserved for Sundays and special occasions.

Goat's milk and sheep's cheese from grass-fed animals provide the calcium needed for maintaining healthy bones.

A vegetarian diet, ensures an adequate intake of healthy fats from nuts, plant oils, and avocados. A small percentage of individuals follow a pescatarian diet, eating seafood in moderation.

UBUNTU

• *Health & Wellness*

"So many people spend their health gaining wealth, and then have to
spend their wealth to regain their health"
A. J. Reb Materi

In many of our prior **THEO*ism*** conversations, we skirted around the health & wellness topic. We will address it in a more holistic way here.

THEO*ism* health & wellness Conversations help participants to become permanent members of the wellness industry by empowering them with the information necessary to become masters of *The Universe Within* (themselves).

•**THEO*ism*** Truth #1 - The reason we can use an electronic thermometer to read our body temperature is because we are energy & vibration.

•**THEO*ism*** Truth #2 - The reason we can use a machine to monitor blood pressure is because we are energy & vibration.

• **THEO*ism*** Truth #3 - The reason why during a hospital stay, a medical attendant can monitor our vital signs is because we are energy & vibration.

THEO*ism* practitioners from all walks of life are asking the same question, what do you feed a sophisticated human-machine whose entire internal operation and communication system is energy and vibration?

Since we are pure energy and vibration, our bodies do not need food; it needs energy, that is why the human body turns food into usable energy.

The human body requires energy. For example, our brains, muscles, and stomach need energy power to function. Our bodies require energy even when we are sleeping.

THEO*ism* practitioners understand that before you can fix or maintain a machine, you must understand its blueprint.

Because we live 24/7, inside of our body, we should know and understand the human blueprint.

The Universe Within is powered, as we mentioned before, by food generated energy.

This food is ingested and digested via our digestive system.

Food is initially mechanically digested in the mouth.

The stomach, intestines, and other parts of the digestive system then chemically digests the food.

Eventually, through diffusion, the glucose and other nutrients are delivered to the mitochondria of our cells.

Here, the glucose is converted to energy via the process known as cellular respiration.

Cellular respiration converts glucose and oxygen into water, carbon dioxide, and usable form of energy (ATP).

Adenosine triphosphate (ATP), an energy-carrying molecule, is found in the cells of all living things.

ATP gathers chemical energy obtained from the breakdown of food molecules and releases it to fuel other cellular processes.

It's important to remember that it usually takes 6-8 hours for food to pass through your stomach and small intestine, and to enter the large intestine, where it becomes fully digested.

The stomach is known as the *Second Brain.*

The enteric nervous system (ENS) is also *known as the* Brain in the Gut because it can operate independently of the Brain, the spinal cord, and the central nervous system (CNS).

It has also been called the "first brain" based on evidence suggesting that the enteric nervous system (ENS) evolved before the central nervous system (CNS).

During one of our **THEO*ism*** conversations, we learnt that the Central Hub or Brain of a system is where all vital information is located.

For example, if you destroy the central Brain or active hub of a web hosting provider, you automatically destroy everything attached to it.

We are aware that, each fetus (unborn baby) is kept alive via its mother's umbilical cord. That cord is attached to that child's Navel (feeding hub), also known as the belly button.

THEO*ism* practitioners branded this belly button our *Central Hub-Brain* because all information, food, blood, and Messages were sent to the child from its mother to that child's *Central Hub-Brain* from which the entire child's development has taken place.

THEO*ism* practitioners explained that the thing we now call our brain, is actually our *Thinking and Reasoning Faculty.*

Our *Thinking and Reasoning Faculty* (the brain), is the hub of our thoughts. It's the interpreter of our external environment. It's the center of control over body movement.

Our belly button is the *Central Hub-Brain* that once connected us to our mother's womb from which we received all the nourishment, signals and messages that led to our development.

Take care of your *Central Hub-Brain* (Gut), and it will take care of your WellBeing.

Based on the above understanding, come with us on our discovery mission in search of the vital role our belly (Gut) plays in our WellBeing.

THEO*ism* practitioners know that our gut can impact the chemistry of our emotions, mood, immune system, and long-term good health.

 Here are some **THEO*ism*** known facts about the Gut that will help you to master *The Universe Within*.

Our "GUT" has more than 100 million brain cells. The Gut is wired to think for itself with millions of neurons in its coils.

That is why our Gut does not need input from the Brain.

When we study the blueprint of *The Universe Within*, we learn another fascinating fact, and that is, the Gut has its nervous system called the enteric nervous system that controls the digestion and elimination process.

Listen to this fascinating discovery. The Gut has a direct connection to the brain called the vagus nerve that carries information one way only, and that is from the Gut to the brain, which the brain interprets as emotions.

That's why our learned Ancestors always said that we should trust our Gut Feelings.

Serotonin is a vital chemical and neurotransmitter, and over 90% is located in our Gut.

Serotonin is believed to help regulate appetite, sleep, mood and social behavior, digestion, memory, and sexual desire.

That is why diet, antibiotics, and medications can harm our mood patterns.

There is also evidence that a healthy Gut could lead to strong bones.

Before we continue, I would like to pause for a few seconds for us to acknowledge the vital role our Guts has in our WellBeing.

Our Gut is more than a food digesting processing system.

The Brain is not the only part of our body that can become addicted to Opiate; our Gut has its opiate receptor, making our Gut capable of addiction to Opiate.

I can recall the day when **THEO*ism*** practitioners found out that our Gut is the home of 70+ percent of our immune cells call lymphoid tissue or Galt which kills and expels virus, bacterium, or other microorganisms (pathogens) that can cause diseases.

Today, we are very conscious of the vital role that our Gut (belly) plays in our WellBeing.

Stomach Acid - The role low stomach acid plays in our overall WellBeing is another critical phase to understanding *The Doctor Within*.

Stomach acid (gastric acid), is indispensable for the digestive process.

When the stomach cannot produce sufficient acid, vital minerals and proteins can't be absorbed into the body.

Balanced stomach acid is necessary for the killing of harmful bacteria from foods and neutralizing enzymes.

Low stomach acid prevents food and nutrients from breaking down, which is the cause for bacterial build up in the stomach, and this leaves the body vulnerable to many diseases and health complications.

Inadequate levels of stomach acid are associated with several health conditions, including Acid reflux, malnutrition, upset stomach, heartburn, nausea, skin issues, osteoporosis, diabetes, asthma, rheumatoid arthritis.

Another lesson we learned is that fermented vegetables have probiotic effects that improve digestion, fight harmful bacteria, and reduce inflammation from low stomach acid.

Studies also show that fermented vegetables are associated with lowering blood pressure, improving our immune system, and weight loss.

To improve our low stomach acid level, we should take small bites and thoroughly chew our food.

Fruits and vegetables increase our stomach acid levels, while processed foods and sugar can cause inflammation in our stomach.

THEO*ism* practitioner learnt an age old secrets that apple cider vinegar is a fermented liquid made from yeast, crushed apples, and bacteria.

Rich in proteins and enzymes, it helps to breakdown bacteria in food. Raw apple cider vinegar can increase stomach acid levels because its acidic properties introduce more acid into the digestive tract.

Please note that apple cider vinegar can damage the enamel of your teeth, it should be diluted in water and drank before a meal.

THEO*ism* practitioners adopted a plant-based food diet that, when converted into energy fuel, it is easily absorbed by the cells.

In many of our casual **THEO*ism*** conversations, we had discussed how Herbalife founders understood the importance of cellular nutrition when they created a product called c*ell activator* that helps the body perform at its best by aiding with the absorption and assimilation of essential nutrients, and it contributes to our body's energy production process.

Our Gut is not only a food processing system; its the Brain that controls our WellBeing.

Take care of our Gut, and it will become our 24/7 doctor, protector, energy builder, and the keeper of our well energized immune defense system.

• Keep Your Cells Energized

Cellular nutrition is based on the principle that our WellBeing depends on how efficient our cells are functioning, and how our lifestyle and diet has a direct effect on our cells and Immune Defense System.

• Plant Based Diet

THEO*ism* practitioners have adopted a plant-based diet that includes; vegetables, fruits, nuts, whole grains, and legumes, and others occasionally consume fish, meat, or dairy products.

It is a well-documented fact that people who eat plant-based diets tend to have a lower body mass index (BMI).

In one of our **THEO*ism*** conversations, we shared The American Heart Association statement that said, eating less meat can also reduce the risk of high blood pressure, high cholesterol, obesity, stroke, and type 2 diabetes.

• Benefits of Alkaline Water

Drinking water generally has a PH level of 7 while Alkaline water typically has a PH level around 7.5 - 9.

Alkaline water molecules are smaller and more readily absorbed by our cells, which helps our body to re-hydrate quickly.

Alkaline water is purported to have various minerals such as calcium and magnesium, which are important for healthy bones.

Alkaline water helps to neutralize the acidity in our bodies by lowering extra acidic content in our gastro-intestinal tract and in the stomach.

• Side Effects of Alkaline Water

One of the side effects is that while it may be alkalizing our body, there is a chance that excessive consumption may ruin the natural acids of our stomach killing the good bacteria.

Furthermore, excessive alkalinity in our body may cause problem in the gastrointestinal tract and skin.

• Natural Healing Remedies

THEOism practitioners *welcome and practice many of the ancient natural healing sciences that nature has revealed to our brothers and sisters from all walks of life!*

• Natural Benefits of Qi Gong

Qi Gong aims to promote the movement of Qi (energy) in the body; this is done by opening energy gates and stretching and twisting energy channels.

51

THEO*ism* practitioners use Qi Gong because it helps them to understand that there is only one breath manifesting in various dimensions, forms, and shapes.

It opens a world of possibilities to communicate physically or spiritually, because nature, as you know, is one uninterrupted energy and vibration, we call the Breath of Life.

The cosmic mind (God) is one seamless breath of life energy and vibration, and a critical point in Qi Gong practice is relaxation and deep breathing, both of which are prerequisites to allow Qi (Life Energy) to flow.

• Natural Benefits of Tai Chi

THEO*ism* practitioners embrace and practice Tai Chi to cultivate the Qi or life energy within us to flow smoothly and powerfully throughout the body.

Tai Chi integrates the mind, body through healthy qi.

Tai Chi benefits include increased energy, improved flexibility, better stamina, excellent balance and agility, better muscle strength, and improved mood.

Many individuals have contributed to their enhanced immune system, their lower blood pressure, quality of sleep, and their overall WellBeing to their embracing and practicing Tai Chi.

• Natural Benefits of Reiki

Reiki is two Japanese words. 'Rei' meaning 'God's wisdom or the 'Higher Power' and 'Ki' meaning 'life force energy.'

Reiki treats the body, emotions, mind, and spirit.

Reiki is a method of spiritual healing and self-improvement.

• Natural Benefits of Yoga

Yoga is known for its ability to ease stress, decrease anxiety, and promote relaxation.

Yoga also helps in the reduction of inflammation, lower blood pressure, and improve breathing.

• Natural Benefits of Acupuncture

Acupuncture stimulates specific anatomic sites commonly referred to as acupuncture points, or acupoints to enhance the natural body, self healing process and functioning of the body.

The standard method used to stimulate acupoints is the insertion of fine, sterile needles into the skin.

• Natural Benefits of Meditation

Meditation training improves a wide range of willpower
skills, including attention,
focus, stress management, impulse control,
and self-awareness.

It changes both the function and structure
of the brain to support self-control.

• Natural Benefits of Daily SunBath

Can you imagine that our entire body is a very
sophisticated solar panel, and once we expose it to the Sun,
it automatically starts to make vitamin D?

Please note that melanin is a natural
sun-blocker.

It protects you from the damaging
Ultra Violet (UV) rays emitted from
the sun.

The darker your skin, the longer it
will take your exposure to the Sun to produce vitamin D.

Do not run from the Sun, *Welcome It!*

Sunbathing reduces blood pressure, it helps to improve
blood circulation, eliminates toxins from the body,
facilitates the bones in the absorption of calcium.

Sunbathing has a massive impact on mild depression.

• Natural Benefits of Deep Breathing

Deep breathing is one of the natural ways of reducing stress, pain, anxiety, high blood pressure.

It stimulates the lymphatic system by detoxifying the body, increase energy, it improve your immune system, improves digestion and blood pressure, and it also helps with your posture.

• Medicinal Laughter

The art of medicine consists of amusing the patient while nature cures the disease.

VOLTAIRE

THEO*ism* practitioners are encouraged to read the book entitled "*Anatomy of an Illness*" by Norman Cousins who was able to cure himself from a deadly disease by taking large amounts of vitamin C and a whole lot of laughter.

Come with us on the journey and discovery of *medicinal laughter.*

Norman Cousins describes his rigorous recovery from Ankylosing Spondylitis.

A painful collagen illness that rendered him immobile, and at its nadir, nearly incapable of moving his jaw.

His doctor and long time friend Dr. William Hitzig put it to him bluntly: only one of every five hundred people diagnosed with this affliction fully recovers.

To beat these odds, he quickly decided he needed to actively pursue why his body was reacting the way it was, and how to reverse the damage.

Foremost, he concluded that a recent, extremely stressful trip to Russia due to miscommunications and tight scheduling had rendered his immune system vulnerable to the toxic fumes emitted by large diesel truck engines working round-the-clock at his hotel.

Then the task before him was simple. He needed to restore his immune system.

He just needed to figure out how.

Relying on previously read books on the subject, such as Hans Selye's *The Stress of Life*, he learned that negative emotions, such as frustration or suppressed rage, are linked to adrenal exhaustion.

Therefore, Cousins assumed the opposite to be true, that positive emotions love, hope, faith, laughter, confidence would yield salutary results.

However, Cousins knew that putting positive emotions to work is nothing as simple as turning on a garden hose.

The pain medication he was administered, roughly 38 pills of aspirin and phenylbutazone per day, he learned could, even in small amounts, be destructive and promote internal bleeding. For this, he requested two things from Dr. Hitzig.

To repair his immune system, dangerously high doses of ascorbic acid or vitamin C, which he read, could combat inflammation and nurture his deteriorating adrenal glands.

And to combat the unbearable pain, Marx brothers films.

Candid Camera and selections from E.B. White's
Subtreasury of American Humor.

He quickly discovered that merely ten minutes of induced
hearty laughter would produce about two hours of painless
sleep.

Laughter decreases stress hormones and increases immune
cells and infection-fighting antibodies, thus improving your
resistance to disease.

Laughter triggers the release of endorphins, the body's
natural feel-good chemicals. Endorphins promote an
overall sense of well-being and can even temporarily
relieve pain.

The result is clear. After several years of continuous
laughter therapy, Cousins experienced little to no pain in
day-to-day living.

Though he relied on vitamin C to physically repair the
immune system, he relied on the often overlooked
medication of laughter to mentally cure his condition.

While psychologists are still researching laughter and its
many health benefits, we don't need to be experts to realize
what a good laugh does to our overall mood.

Laughing is the cheapest form of therapy and by far the
most pleasant one. It has the power to heal not only your
soul but also your body.

Remember how you felt the last time someone left you in tears after cracking a joke? There is no better feeling.

I love laughing and do whatever I can to get my fair share every single day, even if that means watching a short stand-up comedy show or some funny animal compilation.

I need it to distract my mind from dwelling on negative things that happen now and then. And it works every time.

Laughter might be the only contagious thing that you want to catch.

So laugh whenever you get the chance, and laugh hard even when people give you funny looks.

The right kind of person will start laughing too, without even knowing why.

UBUNTU

• *Prayer*

Beliefs and Ideologies Affects Our State of Mind,
Which Can Have A Direct Effect On Our WellBeing
Theo Chambers

THEO*ism* Practitioners believe that prayer should not be asking the creator, whomever you consider God to be, for favors or intervention in the crisis created by humans as a result of man's violation of *Nature's Laws of Existence.*

When one studies and understands nature's fundamental laws of existence for a perfect coexistence among all living things, **THEO*ism*** practitioners don't create individual or prayer groups when faced with adversities and challenges of life.

We find a quiet space where we can communicate with the Doctor and God within for answers to the root causes of our present conditions? And what are some possible solutions?

The Ancestors within in collaboration with the cosmic mastermind will virtually communicate and send us their solutions.

How we interpret and the time we take to implement those solutions will determine the outcome we will experience.

THEO*ism* conversations are deep-rooted in the Socratic principles.

We are not afraid to question our own beliefs and ideologies.

For example, there is a hurricane coming towards the Caribbean, and the entire region is preparing and praying to God to spare them.

Well, the hurricane bypassed Jamaica and destroyed Barbados.

We are now hearing Jamaicans saying that God did answered their prayers.

THEO*ism* practitioners always take those statements to the next level by asking, if your account is correct, then, God ignored the prayers from the Barbadians, and knowingly destroyed their entire island.

THEO*ism* practitioners developed an analytical mind that is always in search of exact causes and effects.

Because of that, we learned that the three main components critical to the formation of a hurricane are warm water, moist warm air, and light upper winds.

We also learn that hurricane begins when large masses of warm water and moist warm air come in contact with cooler air.

This type of analytical approach to disasters and other daily life challenges creates a practical understanding and solutions.

Please note that **THEO*ism*** practitioners believe that there is a significant difference between praying to a deity to intervene and help to resolve health and social problems or to provide some type of material items like a home, car, or other things.

There are prayers and meditation that focus on *The Universe Within.*

The energy and vibration from those prayers can be so powerful that they are capable of waking up the Ancestors within.

This type of prayer/meditation is asking *Nature's Cosmic Laws* to revealed its secrets to you so you can make rational decisions and implement effective solutions.

Let us go back to the above hurricane Example.

THEO*ism* practitioners concluded that the reason why Barbados suffered such a devastating loss, it is not due to God ignoring their prayers, Barbados suffered major catastrophe because they have inferior building code.

If Barbados' building code were half of Jamaica's building codes, the majority of their buildings and airports would still be standing.

The United States building codes need a total overhaul.

Structures are collapsing like paper because many hurricanes and tornado-prone regions are not making it mandatory to build with steel infrastructure.

THEO*ism* practitioners support the concept that prayer is a powerful stimulus to awaken the energy and vibration within, not to control and manipulate *Nature's Laws*.

Another unwritten **THEO*ism*** belief is that the principle of Near Field Communication (NFC) is a compelling human trait.

Reiki, Acupuncture, Group Meditation, Group Training, Live Concerts, Seminars, and other such services and events are the ideal environment where groups (crowd) get their energy and excitement from each other.

This is what we call Near Field Communications (NFC).

Our proximity to each other in those settings triggers an energy (signal) that automatically engulfs those close to us.

For example, when one person start clapping, those close by start to clap also.

If a few person start dancing at a concert, others just join in. It's a domino effect.

Another evidence of the power of Near Field Communication applications is that there is proof that we can change the molecules in water based on the way we think.

THEO*ism* practitioners do not believe that any human has the power to change the molecules or the ebb and flow of the ocean, but they sure can change the molecule of the glass of water they are holding.

Did you know that the mood of plants can be influenced by our thoughts?

Even though **THEO*ism*** practitioners believe that prayer and meditation have powerful energy & vibration qualities, they do not participate in prayers or meditation that passes on to any deity to do for them what they should and can do for themselves.

• The Different Stages of Prayer

THEOism conversations teach it's practitioners to think logically and to break down each step to its most common denominator.

Come with us to one of our **THEO*ism*** Coaching Conversations.

A phone call went out to a religious congregation that their minister took ill and is not doing well.

That call immediately triggered their prayer group who started to pray for his speedy recovery.

During these prayer sessions, the Minister is holding his Bible in one hand and his medical card in his other hand.

Few days later, the word is, he got worst. *Prayer is now over.* Time to go to phase 2, activate the medical card by rushing the Minister to the hospital.

While at the hospital, the prayer has now moved to phase 2.

The Prayer Group is no longer asking God to CURE their Minister because phase 1 failed.

They are now asking God to guide the hands and experience of the doctor.

Good news, the operation went well, and the minister recovered, and the entire prayer group knows for a fact, it was God's intervention.

According to the prayer group, the doctor's experience and skill had nothing to do with the success of the operation.

No one cares at this point that the surgeon was a Jew, Moslem, or an atheist.

They now know that their biblical, Christian God was able to influence the hands and mind of that atheist doctor during the operation. What an imagination!

Now let us look at the opposite side of the same coin.

Bad news, the Minister did not survive the operation, the entire prayer group's actual words are, God is the only one who knows why he called the Minister home at this time.

Others are now saying that he is in a better place. He is out of his pain and suffering.

In none of the above phases of prayer, did any member of the group admit that their prayers were not answered.

They only take credit when there are positive results and when there are negative results it is put on God's shoulders by saying, only God knows why it ended this way.

If the truth is to be told, The Minister was overweight.

He seems to be walking around with a nine months baby in his stomach for the last six years, and he refused to maintain the strict diet his doctors and elders prescribed for him.

Those are the facts. We should not be begging our creator (God) to help us solve problems created by our actions and lifestyle.

THEO*ism* practitioners believe that praying for material favors and health and wellness intervention is deeply rooted in the fact that we are passing our moral and social obligations on to a deity (God) to do our job.

• Business Opportunity Prayers

Even though the majority of successful entrepreneurs around the world contribute their success to sound business strategies, able to fill a void, and having a laser-focused passion, there exists a group of successful entrepreneurs who contribute their success to the intervention of their creator (God).

THEO*ism* practitioners continue to ask themselves, why would God pause his or her *Cosmic Fiduciary Duties* to help humans be financially successful in a niche market, created by man, to satisfy human's fantasy world of fame and glory?

THEO*ism* practitioners accept that the coronavirus is a measuring yardstick to prove beyond a shadow of a doubt, that while businesses are locked down, we have been living for the last few months in a global ghost town, while nature is flourishing.

The absence of human's day to day interaction is having a positive effect on *Planet Earth*.

Our self-imposed lockdown should be a warning and stimulus to help us to humble ourselves, and to accept the indisputable truth; finally, we are not *Planet Earth's Rulers!*

Planet Earth is not our exclusive playground! We are transient vacationers on planet earth, whose passports have an expiration date.

• Prayer Cannot Manipulate Nature's Law

THEO*ism* practitioners understand and acknowledge that at present, man is only using 10% of his brain.

When man can tap into more of his brain resources, the possibility of his power is limitless, but for now, here are the facts.

There is no individual prayer or prayer groups who can influence or manipulate nature or the future. If that were possible, we would all be living in an unpredictable world.

THEO*ism* practitioners acknowledge that the human brain is the most powerful computer on *Planet Earth* to date.

It is innovative, creative, and can think in the past, present, and future.

What the human brain cannot do at this time, is to mentally or via prayer, control, manipulate, or change the outcome of *Nature's Laws* or the future.

Nature is not in the business of granting special favors to those who ask of it.

Human active deforestation activities are noticeable worldwide.

We continue to pollute the air and the water reservoirs.

We invade our bodies with chemicals, junk foods, and we are creating medicine with significant side effects.

Inquisitive prayers that are in search of finding the master keys to nature's building blocks are the prayers that are leading humans to be able to dissect their existence.

Today, we can perform brain and heart surgeries.

Telemedicine is now a reality. 5G technology is about to be integrated into our daily lives, and all this is made possible by taking the time to understand the creator's (God's) blueprint of creation.

Majority of successful people did not relinquish their passion, vision and burning curiosity to accomplish to a deity.

Humans are becoming creators in their own rights by duplicating (mimicking) *The Creator (God) Precise Mathematical Blueprint of Creation.*

THEO*ism* conversations always acknowledge the hidden power of *The Universe Within* each human.

Each one of us is the master of our destiny; therefore, never look down on another person unless you are picking that person up!

We do not need to pray for others; what we need to do is to help each other to activate *The Doctor and God* that is within each of us from birth.

If we accept our first breath of life as the breath of the creator, then God exists within us 24/7, even though we cannot see or touch the oxygen (The Creator's Life Force) that is keeping us alive.

If humans can find quiet moments where they can travel internally through prayer and meditation, they will realize that there is no need to ask the Creator (God) for anything.

We came onto this *Earthly Planet* with all the POWER of the Creator we will ever need to perform miracles beyond verbal explanation.

THEO*ism* practitioners do not believe that there are any lost souls on *Planet Earth.*

If there are lost souls, by which standard are we judging or clarifying people by? How gave us the authority to judge who is a saved or lost soul?

Each living human being lives in their *Internal Mental World*, which no one can visit or experience except that person.

We can have similar experiences, but no one can live and experience *The Universe Within.*

THEO*ism* practitioners have integrated into their daily lifestyle the principle that man is responsible for the making of his living conditions on earth.

Based on our human actions, we are creating heaven or hell or *Earth.*

We cannot find happiness until we create happiness.

There is no possible way of finding joy unless we create joy.

There is no way of finding love, laughter, and peace unless we create love, laughter, and friendship.

We should not pity, degrade, or underestimate *The Doctor and God within* each one of us.

We all have our part to play. Please read our next conversation on success to have a better understanding of *The Universe Within*.

UBUNTU

• *Success*

Success is the quality of life you experience, minus all your earthly possessions
Theo Chambers

In one of our past conversations, we spoke about a good friend of **THEO*ism*** whose awards, diplomas, citations, and pictures of him with celebrities beautifully hanged on his office wall.

His transitory vacation on *Planet Earth* came to a sudden end.

When I went over to his home, a state of sadness took over my entire mind, body, and soul when I saw all those certificates, citations, books, and other items in a box lying in a corner.

That day, those items meant nothing to anyone but my spiritual brother, who transitioned.

Then I asked the *Doctor and God within*, what is success?

And like a lightning bolt, all the communication receptors in my brain lit up with answers from the *Ancestors Within*.

The voice of one of those Ancestors said that success is the quality of life you experience, minus all your earthly possessions.

Then, I remembered witnessing every month, thousands of prosperous and many ultra-rich people coming to Jamaica to relax.

No big house, no BMW, no designer clothes, no Rolex watches, just plain old living life to its most common denominator.

Here are some prophetic words our departing visitors shared with us: "I *cannot wait to come back." "This was one of the best times my family and I had all year."*

Another ancestor voice whispered to me that success is being comfortable with who you are, right where you are.

Another voice said that if you are sad, that means you are living in the past. If you are worried and concerned, that means you are living in the future, and if you are comfortable and relaxed, there is an excellent possibility you are living and enjoying the present moment.

In one of our **THEO*ism*** conversations, we slightly touched on the 2020 Coronavirus.

We mentioned that the entire *earthly world is a ghost town.*

The planet is ok; man's world is in trouble.

For the last two-plus months of the Coronavirus lockdown, what role are the influencers and C-Level executives playing in our day to day living, and business decisions?

Where is the audience that celebrities need to show off their designer clothes, custom made jewelry, and automobiles?

Let us share with you another observation we discovered during many of our **THEOism** conversations.

Many women shared with us how they found their ideal husband, lover, boyfriend, and companion who is financially stable, fun-loving, and intelligent.

They all now have a beautiful home, a new BMW, shopping money, and an impressive diamond wedding ring.

Six months or more into this world of luxury and success, a few realized that her freedom was gone.

She feels that she now needs permission to stay out late with her friends like she used to.

She cannot go anywhere without giving her so-called ideal mate a detailed report of who she is meeting with, and the list of frustrations are endless.

In less than one year, many of them walked away from everything, gave back the big diamond ring, and are now happily living in a one or two bedroom-apartment.

These ladies' experiences of what success means is an inspiration for those who want to know the real difference between material prosperity and spiritual happiness.

Blessed are those who can experience both material and spiritual success.

I am blessed to be able to enjoy simultaneously, personal happiness and the material world and I give credit to my wife, soulmate and confidant, Sharon Oshun Chambers for making that possible.

For us to be able to experience and enjoy simultaneously, personal happiness and the material world, our spiritual being must flow seamlessly and live permanently in our daily consciousness mind.

When we face the truth of life and accept realities such as, how is it that the Creator (God) allows countries that practice Atheisms like China, Japan, Norway, and many others to be at the top of the business chain.

How come, individual atheists listed below are successful, and the majority of devoted religious practitioners are not?

Here is a shortlist of successful atheist, many of whom we admire and love: Richard Branson, Bill Gates, Warren Buffett, Neal DeGrasse Tyson, Stephen Hawkins, George Clooney, Ted Turner, Brad Pitt, Elon Musk, Andrew Carnegie, Edgar Allen Poe, Ernest Hemingway, Angelina Jolie, and Benjamin Franklin.

What we found out is that the majority of them learned how to separate their religious and spiritual dogma, from their business and entrepreneurship-focused passion.

They were able to master *The Universe Within* by listening to motivational speakers like: Les Brown, Anthony Robbins, Deepak Chopra, Earl Nightingale, Jack Canfield, Robert Kyosaki, Wayne Dyer, Jim Rohn, Zig Ziglar, Daymond John, Dale Carnegie, and Barack Obama.

THEO*ism* practitioners do not ask their spiritual and cosmic mind (God) to help them succeed in business because by doing so, we are asking the Creator (God) to participate in a human-designed game of life.

Do we truly believe that the Creator of the Universe has spare time to be actively involved in our daily human activities?

Do you believe that our Creator gives preferential treatment in our business and social affairs to those who pray to him for those favors?

Do you believe that the Creator of this beautiful Universe cares which political party wins? Which artiste wins the Oscar? Which company gets the loan or grant? Which entrepreneurs are allowed to accumulate billions of dollars?

THEO*ism* practitioners admit to themselves that it was man (not God) who created land ownership rules and regulations that prohibit anyone from eating freely of the mango, banana, apple, or grape trees that grows freely in nature.

It was man (not God) who invented the term and system of entrepreneurship, banking, investment, and our tax system.

It was man (not God) who created housing and country clubs. It was also humans who created retirement and determined at what age one can retire.

Based on those truths, **THEO*ism*** practitioners do not mix their cosmic world with their business world.

What does that mean?

THEO*ism* practitioners do not ask their business associates to help them with their Cosmic duties and responsibilities, and they do not ask their infinite soul (God) to help them with their entrepreneurial or business ventures.

There are *Cosmic Laws* that we must follow to be in harmony with nature and *The Universe Within*, and there are a set of *Business and Entrepreneurship Laws* that teaches us how to run a business or how to find employment.

Our universal Cosmic Laws and our Business & Entrepreneurship Laws are like oil and water; they will never and should never mix.

THEO*ism* practitioners and coaches are conscious of the fact that many businesses and entrepreneurs are tapping into our cosmic and spiritual world by dissecting and analyzing the building blocks of the *Cosmos*.

THEOism practitioners believe that man cannot destroy the Cosmos.

Man can manipulate, re-arrange many of nature's formulas.

Still, if humans go too far, then, *Mother Earth* will create a hostile environment that will cause humans to self-eliminate themselves from planet earth before their earthly transitory vacation passport expires.

We do not need to pray and remind the creator that he needs to intervene before it's too late. Pure energy and vibration (The Creator) is always in control.

It's ridiculous for humans to think that the life force which created us (God), need us to remind it that many of our fellow brothers and sister are destroying the planet.

If you think that CoronaVirus is not part of such intelligence, then, we need to study and understand the *Cosmic Laws of Creation and Existence.*

Have you noticed that the CoronaVirus is not causing massive deaths among other animal species except humans?

Back to our success conversation.

When our *planetary transitory vacation passport expires,* and we are deported penniless back from whence we came, what is going to happen to all of our *Earthly* material possessions?

Money in the bank? Our automobiles? Our properties and Land? Our clothes and jewelry? Our chairmanship, presidency, stocks, and shares?

It is wise to let the pleasure of giving and sharing of our material possessions to be ours, instead of having those items be given away in our name after we take our last breath.

THEO*ism* practitioners noticed that the transitioning of great bygone inventors, leaders, religious scholars, earthly named saints, and loving families, friends, and associates into Ancestryhood, did not have any effect whatsoever on mother nature's daily routine.

Coronavirus pandemic lockdown is showing us that *Planet Earth* can and will function fine without the active operation of corporations, manufacturing plants, influencers, trade shows, outdoor events, airplanes, and automobiles.

Based on the impact of the Coronavirus, **THEO*ism*** practitioners are one hundred percent (100%) convinced that all the above businesses and social activities were designed for our earthly experiences and joy.

In reality, our business and social lifestyle has nothing to do with *Nature's Laws* and the *Cosmos Mathematical Principles of Cause & Effect.*

UBUNTU

• *Ignorance Is No Excuse*

*Ignorance of the law is no excuse in any country. If it were,
the laws would lose their effect,
because it can always be pretended.*
Thomas Jefferson

THEO*ism* practitioners acknowledge that ignorance of the *Cosmic, Earthly Planetary and Worldly Laws* is no excuse.

We must accept responsibility for any laws that we consciously or unconsciously violate.

• Ignorance Explained

THEO*ism* practitioners and coaches are amazed when they listen to individuals who display self-righteousness by claiming to be saved.

Others claimed to have lived an honest and clean life.

In contrast, others claimed they are so righteous that they now devote their lives trying to save others, even though Jesus, Buddha, Confucius, and other prophets never in their entire lives went out to try to convert non-believers.

If that statement is true, where did we humans get the authority to deprive God (creator of the universe) of his prerogative to punish unbelievers because we human took the responsibility unto ourselves to punish in the name of God those we deem to be unbelievers or need to be saved?

As long as our earthly transitory passport is still active, and we live and participate in society's daily activities, we are all co-conspirators to everything that is happening on *Planet Earth*, good or bad.

For example, we have a moral obligation to respect nature's laws by protecting the rainforest, which is a vital player in keeping the balance of the ecosystem.

When we purchase our acre of land and build our beautiful home (nothing wrong with that), we reduced the capacity of that area to absorb carbon dioxide that contributes to climate warming and other environmental challenges.

Some of the money we paid to the construction team could be going towards the purchase of drugs and other criminal activities, and a significant portion might go towards noble causes.

Ignorance of how our payments are used, should be no excuse to exonerate us from being an innocent co-conspirator.

Regardless of how it was spent, our payment contributed to the end results of each of the above instances.

This rude awakening should knock us off of our Self Glorification Pedestal, causing us to be less judgmental.

An innocent co-conspirators are not in contradiction or an excuse not to punish those who knowingly violate our environmental laws or viciously commit crimes against other humans, animals, or nature.

If we operate a restaurant and one of our main courses includes steak or pork, we might not be aware of how those animals are slaughtered.

 If there is any cruelty towards animals in our chain supply, our ignorance should not be an excuse from blame because we are an active participant in that network of supply and demand.

When we join and pledge allegiance to a religious, political, business, or social institution that claims to be the *Real McCoy*, aren't we directly or indirectly guilty of promoting separatism and discrimination?

Instead of accepting different views and conclusions based on the same source of information, we find ways to explain why our interpretation is more genuine. We reject blindly opposition views.

There is no doubt that they are ideologies and systems that should be rejected because they suppress other's freedom to live and to enjoy life regardless of one's race, age, gender, religious dogma, political affiliation or institutional academic accomplishment.

How can we isolate ourselves from this worldly chaotic yet beautiful and challenging daily interactions we experience and be unaware that we are a seamless active participant in this *Earthly Human Web* of love, hate, jealousy, racism, and selfishness to mention a few?

When we vote for a political leader, we are endorsing the ideology and philosophy of that person that might be in harmony with our views, which are directly in opposition to the other party or parties' views or ideology.

Voting seldom leads to the merger of opposite party agenda.

It always leaves the wishes of others unfulfilled.

Yes, our vote did contribute to someone winning and others losing for which we should take full responsibility.

This **THEO*ism*** conversation's goal and objective is to highlight that our actions consciously or unconsciously are contributing to every phase of society, and we should not feel that our activities and crimes are lesser and more acceptable than those of others.

THEO*ism* practitioners accepts the truth that when we came into this world, there was no book of instructions that came from our mother's womb that explained our roles and responsibilities.

We are still responsible for our actions because, each one of us was born with a direct link to the *Cosmic Master Mind of Creation.*

All animals and plants possess the same uninterrupted linkages to the creator's pure energy & vast vibrations resource (library) of cause and effect solutions to which our Ancestors have answers.

Since we are the living repository of our Ancestors, all we have to do is to tap into *The Universe Within* and start a conversation with those *Ancestors*.

For example, birds were born with the knowhow to create a bird's nest.

All animals were born with built in mating instinct.

All animals, including humans, were born with their fight or flight instinct of survival.

When we sit quietly like many of our great *Ancestors* have done, we can learn so much about who we are and our genuine relationship with planet earth.

We must, therefore, take full responsibility for our worldly environment and quietly asking ourselves the following:

How many families have been destroyed because of religious, political, or social differences?

How many of us try to dictate or decide who a family member or friend should date or marry?

How many of us object to inter-racial marriages?   How many of us object to inter-cultural relationships?

How many of us object to marrying anyone outside of our religious faith?

How many of us have done favors for friends even though others were more qualified or in need?

How many times have we gotten special treatment because we knew someone or a friend or family member had those connections?

How many people during our lifetime have we deprived of opportunities because of our friendships or network associations?

Can humans sincerely live and actively participate within our worldly business, political, or social environment without violating basic principles of fairness or morality?

Let us try our best to be more aware of the impact of our actions throughout the entire value chain.

We should try not to be judgmental, or walk around with our academic, business and political achievements as a passport to look down on others because we are guilty of so many crimes that are downright immoral and unfair to others.

Pretending or claiming to be unaware of those ramifications is no excuse because we have established that ignorance of the law is no excuse!

UBUNTU

• *Sleep Towards The South*

Sleep Is A Rehearsal For Death
I Enjoy My Peaceful & Restful Nights
Theo Chambers

THEO*ism* practitioners and coaches understand the power of Rest (quality sleep), and what are some of the things we need to know and do to have a positive and energetic Rest?

To understand the cosmic laws of restfulness (quality sleep), we should examine the plant world to understand the human internal photosynthesis process.

During day time (sunshine), *plants* perform photosynthesis by converting sunlight, water, and carbon dioxide into stored Energy.

During night time (darkness), plants burn their stored starch to fuel continued growth.

Our *Ancestors* learned that *light* prevents the secretion of Melatonin that naturally promotes sleep.

Even while we are sleeping, our bodies won't produce Melatonin if there is light in our sleeping space because light can be detected through our eyelids.

Please note that Melatonin is the human reset button for our body's internal clock.

Hence when it starts to get dark, we feel sleepy because the body automatically starts to produce Melatonin, which induces sleep naturally.

Plants understand the different functions they must perform during the day and at night, while humans take all types of drinks and pills to stay awake instead of following their internal clock.

By not getting the proper rest, the human body is unable to produce melatonin from doing its work as a potent antioxidant, anti-inflammatory, immune modulator.

We are not surprised to know that we are out of balance with *The Universe Within*. We are neglecting the Doctor and God Within.

Today, we know that melatonin supplements can assist people who travel a lot and fight jet lag, night shift workers who have to sleep in the daytime, and those who fight insomnia.

Please consult your doctor if you need melatonin supplements.

THEO*ism* practitioner's research shows that Melatonin could also have Neuroprotective effects by facilitating the control of chronic diseases such as cardiovascular diseases, diabetes, and obesity.

Besides, Melatonin could even regulate mood, sexual maturation, and body temperature.

Any light in our sleeping space at night sends a wakeup message to the brain, suppressing the production of the sleep-inducing hormone melatonin that prevents us from falling asleep.

THEO*ism* practitioners sleep in well-designed space by making sure that there are no artificial or moonlight penetrating their room.

This includes the absence of any technology light such as cellphones, television, even the red light that shows on electronic equipment and computer screen light.

Many of our Practitioners wear a sleeping mask to bed.

It is highly recommended by our *Ancient Ancestors* who understood the oneness of all living things, and the cause and effect they have on each other, that we lie down with our heads pointed towards the South and the feet naturally facing the North.

You can download a compass to your smartphone that can help you to identify north, south, east and west.

The reason sleeping towards the South is essential is because the human head is known to have a polar-like attraction, and it needs to face southward to attract opposite poles while we are resting.

There should be no mirrors, books, no electronics, and no additional items in our sleeping space.

THEO*ism* practitioners believe that in order to have Pure Energy flowing within their sleep environment, their beds are positioned away from doors and windows.

Beds are positioned against a solid wall (pointing south), and NOT put in the center of their room.

They have removed glowing digital clocks from view, and no moonlight or street lights are sharing their sleeping space.

The *Earth's Magnetism* is powerful, and based on this truth, **THEO*ism*** practitioners adopted many of the ancient practices.

The Earth, because its core is filled with iron and spins at high speeds, has a magnetic field that goes from the *North* to the *South*.

Sleeping facing the North Pole, creates a conflict with our body because the human head is also a Positive Pole, which cancels out each other.

According to ancient findings, this type of conflict where *Earthly North Pole* and human *(head)* Positive Pole pointing in the same direction, can affect blood circulation, causes sleeping disorders, nightmares and makes one wakeup feeling not rested.

Even though the majority of **THEO*ism*** practitioners strongly believe that sleeping towards the South allows our *Earthly Energy* to flow positively, others feel that sleeping towards the East, neutralizes the magnetic fields which give them great health benefits, improved memory, and they are able to focus better.

- *The North Pole Shifted*

The North Magnetic Pole moves over time due to magnetic changes and flux lobe elongation in the Earth's core. In 2009, while still situated within the Canadian Arctic at 84°54′N 131°00′W, it was **moving** toward Russia at between 55 and 60 km (34 and 37 mi) per year.

UBUNTU

90

• *Are We Perfect?*

In order to decide what is Perfect or Imperfect, we need to create or agree on what we consider to be a Perfect Specimen, Product or Services
Theo Chambers

THEO*ism* conversations sporadically point out the power, clear vision, and understanding we all possess once we can acknowledge, manage, and execute *The Universe Within*.

THEO*ism* practitioners believe that the *Cosmic Laws* are an endless no beginning and no end recycling *Creation* with new species emerging at various phases of life.

Growing up, all of us have heard others say that its OK to make a mistake because we are not perfect.

THEO*ism* practitioners and coaches have adopted the statement that we live in a *Perfect Chaotic World*; therefore, everything within that world, including humans, are a part of that *Cosmic Precise Mathematical and Perfect Chaotic Universe.*

Please note that the statement I am about to make, I take full responsibility for its accuracy or falseness.

No human has ever witnessed or seen a perfect human being. Since that is true from **THEO*ism*** practitioner's perspective, then, we have concluded that no one can state with any certainty that humans are not perfect.

We cannot state that humans are not perfect if we have no idea what perfect human beings look, behave or think like.

It's somewhat incomprehensible to think that the creator of this *Perfect Chaotic Universe*, including our *Earthly Planet* could end up creating *Imperfect Human Beings!*

Now, if a person designs a business, social, or political system with its own rules and regulations, then, each person would have to learn those rules and regulations in order to participate.

Because someone is unable to accurately learn the system protocols of a company, (rules of the game), that does not make that person imperfect, dumb or useless.

It seems that when we label humans as not being perfect, we are doing so by comparing that person's ability to execute specific business or everyday tasks without mistakes.

If the answer or result was not what we wanted, usually we do not make an effort to find out why we got the result we received; instead, we indirectly blame the creator (God) for not creating perfect human beings by saying, "It's OK, we humans are not perfect."

If humans are not perfect, then, the Creator definitely allowed imperfection in his human design blueprint.

Theo*ism* practitioners reject that belief that humans are imperfect.

THEO*ism* practitioners and coaches acknowledge that every human being is a perfect creation whether the person is blind, deaf, tall or short, black, white, or of Chinese descent, we are all perfect creations.

Did you know that the majority of acupuncture gurus in the East are blind?

By not being able to see, *The Doctor and God Within* were able to give those individuals special *Energy & Vibrational skills* that the average people do not possess.

Autistic individuals (savants) possess extraordinary abilities that the average human being does not have.

THEO*ism* practitioners learnt that about ten percent of individuals with autism show signs of savant talents.

Savant syndrome is a condition which causes many autistic individuals to demonstrate individual skills way beyond what any average person can learn.

Some can tell you in detail what the weather was almost 200 years ago, anywhere in the world.

They can read an entire 500-page book within minutes and remember every detail of the book.

They can tell you who was the President or King of a country 200 years ago. Others can calculate complicated figures faster than a computer.

Some can look at a building for a few minutes and draw that building with detailed precision.

Kim Peek was an extraordinary autistic savant who was able to read with his left eye and his right eye simultaneously, reading pages of text in seconds while retaining about ninety-eight percent of the information.

The above mentioned ninety-eight percent just reminded me that human DNA and those of a chimp is about 98% identical, and the 2% difference makes our communications skills non-compatible.

Which individual was born with the right to decide that the chimp is an imperfect creation, and man is a perfect creation because of our communication and imaginary skills?

Who gives anyone the *Cosmic Power* to analyze, determine, and brand any fellow human as perfect or imperfect?

We are living in a world where the color of one's skin is a determining factor of human perfection.

In a few of our **THEO*ism*** conversations, it was hinted that those who claimed to be the perfect race, each one of them should have their DNA test done and share their perfect family lineages with the world.

What a rude awakening those individuals would have after reading and dissecting their family trees.

THEO*ism* practitioners & Coaches agree that all humans came into the world the same way.

We breathe the same oxygen, and our entire *Universe Within* is laid out and functions the same.

Based on these facts, we are perfect human beings.

How we fit into our *global businesses, social and political worldly structures* (games), has nothing to do with our perfect creation status.

Perfection can duplicate itself in whatever form it wants, and those duplications cannot be imperfect.

Since we are a creation of the *Perfect Universal Cosmic Mastermind* (God), then, we are the product of perfection, which automatically makes us *Perfect Human Beings* that come in all shapes, sizes, colors, energy and vibration.

Plants and animals also come in all colors, shapes and sizes, but we have never developed or branded what is a perfect plant or animal by which all others will be judged, then, why should there be such standards among humans?

In one of our **THEO*ism*** conversations, we stated that if human standards of perfection were created by the fashion and beauty industries, cultural standards created by chiefs and tribal elders, social or political groups, then, those are *Earthly Worldly Standards* that has nothing to do with our perfect creation from pure potentiality into a transitory vacationing earthly planetary physical being.

• Short Stories To Live By

The following are quotations and short stories that can have a positive impact on our health, happiness, self esteem, and the way we experience each day.

• Anger

Anger is the punishment we give ourselves
for someone else's mistake.
Jo Dickinson

When we get angry, we end up giving ourselves migraine headaches, stress, strokes, increased heart rate, blood pressure and even heart attacks, increased respiration, inability to reason, and the brain triggering our fight or flight syndrome.

Why, because of someone else's action, decisions, behavior, or even statement we dislike or that we thought was not truthful.

Can you explain why anyone should punish themselves in such a manner due to someone's or a group of individual's actions that we did not appreciate or agree with?

We have a duty to protect our good health and *WellBeing*, and we must do our best never to allow a third party to cause us health and wellness discomfort or irreparable mental or physical damage.

96

• *Living In The Present*

The secret of health for both Mind and Body is not to mourn for the past, worry about the future, or anticipate troubles, but to live in the present moment wisely and earnestly.
Buddha

We all know that the past will never come back, and when tomorrow shows up, we still call it today.

So, if the past will never return, and the future will never come, and each day the only thing you wake up to is Today, then, if you enjoy all the "Todays" you would have become the master of your destiny.

Think back to all the emergencies, concerns, and worries you have been through your entire life, and today, you are still alive and doing well.

What does that tell you? It says that you have conquered all past challenges, and because of that, you have the formula to conquer all perceived future challenges!

Another coping and self-management tool you have at your fingertip is this, all worries, problems, and challenges can only show up one day at a time called today.

Since you are the master of all your past today's, you will master those daily challenges in the same way you have done for years.

• Your Mental Radio Signal

*It is those who concentrate but on one thing at a time
who advance in the world!*
Og Mandino

When we plug our radio into the electrical socket, or we turn on the radio in our automobile, sometimes we get two stations trying to compete for our attention.

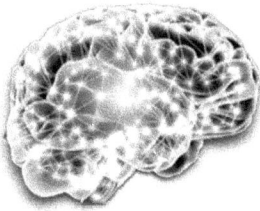

We always do our best to fine-tune our search by selecting the strongest signal for clarity and better listening.

When we select a particular station, it does not change the fact that all the other stations are live and millions of people are tuned into them, but we chose at this time, not to listen to those stations.

The same is true with our modern technology, smartphones and Apps.

There are billions of active websites and Apps, but we can only select one particular website, or App at a time.

The human brain is laid out the same way with millions of live receptors like; happy receptor; angry receptor, compassionate receptor; taste receptor; listening receptor, decision making receptor and a limitless list of receptors that we cannot turn off.

Like radio signals, they are all functioning uninterrupted in the background and the only way you become conscious (aware) of any of those receptors, is when you mentally dial (move) your energy (awareness) to that area of the brain.

Every day of our lives, we allow the newspapers, WhatsApp, Facebook, Twitter, LinkedIn, Newsflash, Fake News, Bills, and our desires to move our energy (awareness) all over our brain, then at the end of the day, we have accomplished nothing.

We have no idea why we feel exhausted and ready to sleep in order to replenish the energy that we wasted all day due to lack of focus on any one item we want to accomplish.

Make a list of the things you would like to accomplish, then, turn your mental dial (energy) to one task (receptor) at a time, do not allow the other stations (other receptors) to divert your attention (awareness/focus) from your present task until it is completed.

Since we seldom know how to say *No* to people whose requests robs us of our finite daily energy, and our inability to say *No* to unproductive meetings and fruitless conversations, let us change those habits and become laser focused on our projects by adopting the prophetic words of wisdom from the founder of Apple, Steve Jobs:

> *Focus does not mean saying yes*
> *It means saying No!*
> Steve Jobs

• *Choose To Stop Suffering!*

*Choose to STOP suffering now by shifting your memory
and imagination to a more positive space*
Sharon Oshun Chambers

Today marks the first day of the rest of your life. Live your life, exert your positive intentions or let life live you and exert its unknown intentions upon you.

Stop suffering by removing lack and limitation from your mind and imagination. You are what you think! Vision yourself the way you want to be. Shift - Focus and Re-Connect to a new Conscious and Visual image of yourself. Make a conscious decision to stop suffering NOW!

Leave yesterday in the dustbin of eternity. Suffering is NOT a way of life. Cancel, Cancel and Cancel all negative thoughts and images.

Transforming the personality takes time. So be patient, begin to consciously Cancel negative thoughts, saying the words: "Cancel, Cancel, Cancel".

With practice, clearing, cancelling negative and repressed thoughts in the subconscious, eventually you will become more positive and harmonious.

Sacred Practice: Stand in front of the mirror and speak to your mirror image. Cross your hands over your heart and gaze into your eyes. Saying: "I love me and I honor me." "I will never allow anyone to hurt or abuse me." "I will never give up on me." "I love my life and enjoy being alive." Then turn it around as if you are the Coach speaking and say: "I love you and I honor you." "I will never allow anyone to hurt or abuse you." "I will never give up on you." "Love the life you life and enjoy yourself."

Smile and visualize the feeling of being loved by your parents, friends and family. Enjoy these vibrations. Repeat as often as necessary.

Affirmation: I choose to Live Life to the Fullest.

• Why Do We Have Government?

In *"These Are the Times That Try Men's Souls"* (1776), Thomas Paine brings clarity to the reason for government. He stated:

"Society in every state is a blessing, but Government, even in its best state is but a necessary evil; in its worst state, an intolerable one: for when we suffer or are exposed to the same miseries by government, which we might expect in a country without government, our calamity is heightened by reflecting that we furnish the means by which we suffer."

Paine further stated: "Here then is the origin and rise of government; namely, a mode rendered necessary by the inability of moral virtue to govern the world."

Wow, can you truly understand that the reason why government exists is due to the fact that we are unable to govern ourselves morally.

Government is like a watchdog, ready to punish us for our wrong doing. Punish us for not keeping our promises or being fair to each other.

So when we complain, we should always remember that we created government to keep our bad behaviors in check.

It even gets more complicated when government becomes the Watchdog and the Bad Dog at the same time.

What a monster (government) we created due to our inability to treat each other morally and fairly!

• What is white privilege?

"There are these two young fish swimming along, and they happen to meet an older fish swimming the other way, who nods at them and says, "Morning, boys, how's the water?" And the two young fish swim on for a bit, and then eventually one of them looks over at the other and goes, "What the hell is water?"

David Foster Wallace

What is white privilege? When a group of individuals are immersed from birth in a particular culture, ideology or lifestyle all the days of their lives, they just exist without once questioning their environment, privileged status, and the effect their lifestyle has on the wider population.

It is when they are taken out of their environment (a fish out of water) the struggle to survive starts, that is when they understand better the struggle of those who have not had the privilege to participate in the ocean of opportunities and success that is so protected by a minority.

People cannot stay immersed in their comfort zone and truly understand the injustice that is being inflicted on the wider population when consciously or unconsciously the system is manipulated to prevent others from becoming part of the ocean of opportunities that a few enjoy so freely.

When I did my 23andMe DNA, I was surprised when I saw these words under my paternal lineages:

You share an ancient paternal lineage with Pharaoh Ramesses III.

Does this give me the right to claim my royal status? Should my paternal lineages to Pharaoh Ramesses III give me bragging rights? Should I get special treatment because I have royal blood running in my veins?

I should not use my family lineage to deprive others of any business, social, or political opportunities.

We must give thanks for the days of the hippies, and to our musicians whose music and lifestyle are influencing the young generation from all walks of life, to the point that the fight for equality is being supported by a diverse group who refuses to adopt their parents' and grandparents' lifestyle of segregation.

The novel Coronavirus and Black Life Matters are changing the world beyond verbal explanation. I am truly optimistic that the change is for the better.

Regardless of our cultural, social, political or religious dogma, we are all part of the human race and its time that we learn to co-exist within the same space under the umbrella and philosophy of **Ubuntu**.

• *Who Are Your Children?*

Your Children Are Not Your Children
Kahlil Gibran

And a woman who held a babe against her bosom said, Speak to us of Children. And he said:

Your children are not your children.

They are the sons and daughters of Life's longing for itself.

They come through you but not from you, and though they are with you they belong not to you.

You may give them your love but not your thoughts,
For they have their own thoughts.

You may house their bodies but not their souls,
For their souls dwell in the house of tomorrow, which you cannot visit, not even in your dreams.

You may strive to be like them, but seek not to make them like you.

For life goes not backward nor tarries with yesterday.
You are the bows from which your children as living arrows are sent forth.

The archer sees the mark upon the path of the infinite, and He bends you with His might that His arrows may go swift and far.
Let your bending in the archer's hand be for gladness;
For even as He loves the arrow that flies, so He loves also the bow that is stable.

• Be Careful of your thoughts

Thought is food. Go now and feast on positive thoughts
Sharon Parris-Chambers

One evening an old Cherokee told his grandson about a battle that goes on inside people. He said, "My son, the battle is between two 'wolves' inside us all.

One is Evil. It is anger, envy, jealously, doubt, sorrow, regret, greed, arrogance, self-pity, guilty, resentment, inferiority, lies, false pride, superiority, and ego.

The other is good. It is joy, peace, love, hope, serenity, humility, kindness, benevolence, empathy, generosity, forgiveness, truth, compassion and faith."

The grandson thought about if for a minute and then asked his grandfather:

"Which wolf wins?"

The old Cherokee simply replied, *"**The One You Feed**"*

• 212° Extra Degree

Many of life's failures are men who did not realize how close they were to success when they gave up
Thomas Edison

At 211° Degrees, water is hot. At 212° degrees, it boils, and with boiling water comes steam, and steam can power a locomotive.

212°
THE EXTRA DEGREE

Now you are conscious of 212° Extra Degree philosophy that states basically that by raising the temperature of water 1° degree, it start to create steam and steam leads to exponential possibilities.

Sometimes with a little extra effort, and perseverance, one is able to accomplish that which looked impossible at the time. Just 1° degree of extra push could make a big difference in your life.

Effective today, make a commitment to yourself that you will always push your plans and projects that extra degree so you can work within the 212° degree or above environment of exponential possibilities.

As a parent, wake up each day with the understanding that your actions will be absorbed by your children, and your children will grow to be contributing adults to the level of your influence.

Imagine the exponential positive effect you will have on your children by spending an extra hour weekly with them?

• Your Teacher

One of the major lessons I have learned in my own personal and spiritual development has been that other people can reflect to me aspects of myself that I need to address, or lessons that I need to learn.
Russell Bishop

Anything that annoys you is for teaching you patience.

Anyone who abandons you is for teaching you how to stand up on your own two feet.

Anything that angers you is for teaching you forgiveness and compassion.

Anything that has power over you is for teaching you how to take your power back.

Anything you hate is for teaching you unconditional love

Anything you fear is for teaching you courage to overcome your fear.

Anything you can't control is for teaching you how to let go and trust the universe.

Jackson Kiddad

• **AI and Human Partnership**

Artificial Intelligence systems don't have feelings. They don't know right from wrong. They only know what they are trained to do. If we train them to steal, to cheat, to disable, to destroy, that's what they will do.
Shelly Palmer

THEO*ism* practitioners understand that *Artificial Intelligence* is a powerful group of technologies that can, and will do extraordinary things, both good and bad.

Even though artificial intelligence (AI) is drastically changing how work gets done and who does it, AI's impact will be working together with consciousness (humans) to double-check for errors, and in increasing human capabilities, not replacing them.

Amazon announced new developer tools to enable Alexa to speak with emotions; it does not change the fact that Alexa is not a person; it is not male or female. It is a machine.

Here are some of the things Alexa is trained to do (not think) to help enhance human productivity:

Alexa's human-like qualities are not limited to; voice interaction, streaming podcasts, playing audiobooks, making to-do lists, setting alarms, music playback, and providing weather, traffic, sports, and other real-time information, such as news.

THEO*ism* practitioners understand that big data can be analyzed to reveal patterns, trends, and associations, especially relating to human behavior and interactions that are too large and sometimes complex to be dealt with by traditional data-processing application software.

AI's ability to work with data analytics is the primary reason why AI and Big Data are inseparable.

AI machine learning and deep learning are learning from every data input and using those inputs to generate new rules for future business analytics.

THEO*ism* practitioners have taken the veil of ignorance from their eyes by accepting the truth that our *privacy* is now history.

Our identity is common knowledge available to anyone who wants to do their homework.

Here is a short list where information can be found publicly on anyone who is actively participating in the workforce, social media, or by owning a smartphone.

Phone books are still a vital source of information on businesses and individuals.

If you own a home or are renting your place of residence (this information is public record available to anyone).

LinkedIn and other social media platforms are other sources of information.

For example, things you like, the food you eat, who are your friends, the type of clothes you wear, all are available from your Instagram or other social media posts.

You cannot get anything free on the internet, including an email address or a social media account without sharing your email, phone numbers, gender, age, and other vital information. ***Privacy?***

Your credit card debt and credit score are available to companies you are seeking a loan from.

THEO*ism* practitioners were not surprised when they learnt that our entire online behavior is giving big data more information to understand better who we are.

Google, Facebook, Instagram, Twitter, LinkedIn all know which website page you visited.

What words you were searching for, how long you spent on a particular page, what you ordered online, which products you looked at but did not buy, and where you are in the world via GPS.

They have an accurate idea of how much time you spent on social media per day, what you post, or reposted.

There is a technology in use, referred to as Automatic Content Recognition that allows TV manufacturers to know what you are watching on cable, satellite, or streaming.

It automatically sends this data every second to the TV manufacturer. They can identify who you are, where you are, and what you're watching.

All of these behaviors are captured, logged, analyzed, and used to enrich your profile 24/7, 365 days per year.

AI is not only gathering and updating our identity profile; Artificial Intelligence is integrated into our day to day lifestyle.

The truth is we are already using AI to enhance our quality of life and have been doing so for years.

We know that man can fit prosthetic arms that are controlled by that person's brainwave.

Today, we know that by hacking the Universe Within (brain), the brain-computer interface has the capability to enhance the daily lives of individuals with prosthetic limbs.

A brain-computer interface (machine interface), is a method that enables an individual to control a computer using only their thoughts.

Individuals are shown how to use a particular thought to flex their knee that creates electrical activities in the nerve cells, and also brainwaves.

A chip can be placed in the brain to detect electrical activity, or electrodes can be positioned on the scalp to identify brainwaves. AI makes CT Scans safer and more informative.

Individuals with amputation or paralysis, can use a brain-computer interface to control the movement of muscles, limbs, and prosthetics.

In one of our previous **THEO*ism*** conversations, we discussed the possibility that one day one of our world leaders or business executive's medical records will be hacked, and inside of his or her records is the manufacturer and model number of their pacemaker.

Empowered with such knowledge, that person or group of individuals are able to write a script that interrupts the operation of that pacemaker, causing that person's instant death.

This lethal attack could quickly be launch via a near field communication signal.

THEO*ism* practitioners are very conscious of the fact that everything created by man, good or bad, was first conceived in *The Universe Within* (mind).

Because our Ancestral DNA is traceable for thousands of years, it knows and remembers how we got here.

THEO*ism* practitioners believe that when we arrived on *Planet Earth*, we came programmed with many functions on automatic pilot like our entire internal operating system from our heart pump, food processing, body temperature, and even childbirth.

Humans also arrived on planet earth with a large portion of their brains like a new video camera, ready to capture new information such as social lifestyle, languages and accents, political ideology, religious dogma, and educational careers.

Our technological innovations were first designed and executed in our *Minds*.

Since everything starts in our *Brain*, we can hack ourselves and extract ancient hidden secrets and share those secrets with other humans in a universal duplicatable mathematical code system and readable language.

We are HACKING our *Brain* and extracting processes faster than we can blink our eyes.

Within ten years or less, humans will have chips implanted in their bodies with limitless functionalities.

THEO*ism* practitioners predict that Amazon Go App (its checkout-free store) will soon implant into humans their checkout-free store chip.

It will allow individuals with the embedded chip to walk into their store, pick up whatever they want, then checkout out by leaving the store.

Amazon's *Artificial Intelligence* knows what you purchased and was able to process your orders the minute you walked out.

Despite moral and religious objections, *Robotic Surgery* is an integral integration in our daily lives.

Each day, man is figuring out how the Creator's (God's) childbirth blueprint was designed, and now they can make nanotechnology robots with features similar to a heat-seeking missile, with specific mission and target within the human body.

They can remotely operate and implement such operation with precision because they got their information directly from the Creator's blueprint by HACKING the most fabulous computer ever known to man, *The Universe Within* (Our Brain).

THEO*ism* practitioners feel that we are now living in the future.

What excites **THEO*ism*** practitioners is that even though we are witnessing technology unfolding before our eyes, the most exciting thing we all are experiencing is how humans are HACKING their evolution and creation, which is self-revealing.

These nature's secrets were not even imaginable twenty or fifty years ago.

Here we are seeing how Consciousness (God) curving back into itself to recreate itself is an infinite unfolding process of creation.

Our fingerprints, eyes, and DNA are unique to each person.

That is why today, Iris (eye) recognition that uses mathematical pattern-recognition techniques on video images of one or both of the irises of an individual's eyes, is use for identification.

Imagine walking into a store, passing through customs, or any public space that has biometric identification cameras installed, and to gain entrance, you just look into the security camera.

Unknown to you, your entire identity pops up.

Think about the day, which is very soon, where police officers can scan your eyes using a portable biometric identification machine that will give them instant results about who you are because of the power of 5G network.

Experts claim that Iris recognition is one of the best biometric modalities in terms of accuracy.

Because of its accuracy, several hundred million persons around the world enrolled in Iris recognition systems for expediency purposes such as passport-free automated border-crossings, and various national ID programs.

Another advantage of Iris recognition is knowing that the Iris' patterns remain stable throughout an individual's life. Because of its stability, the iris recognition system is difficult to forge by any means, making it simple and secure.

THEO*ism* practitioners wrestle with the fact that not only is our *Universe Within* being HACKED, but our moral standards and privacy that we have treasured for so long is also being hacked.

Surveillance Cameras are everywhere.
We can no longer have private meetings or dinner with loved ones or business associates without AI eyes monitoring our every move.

We should not underestimate the decisive role surveillance cameras have played in identifying and capturing criminals and law-breaking individuals.

The reason is that most AI systems are and will be in the hands of companies whose focus is profits or governments whose goal is power.

Our deep-rooted dependency on network artificial intelligence is eroding our ability to think for ourselves, to take action independent of automated systems.

THEO*ism* practitioners ask if morality and privacy is no longer part of our lives, does that mean that transparency is going to be the new norm? If the answer is yes, how do we protect against identity theft?

Individuals like Elon Musk is on the verge of merging humans and technology by promising to insert *Bluetooth* enabled chips into our *brain*, claiming the devices could enable telepathy and repair motor function in people with injuries.

Brain-Chip-Interfaces are Hybrid Settings where chips and nerve cells initiate close physical interactivity allowing the movement of information in one or both directions.
Please note that according to our research,
implantable microchips are not picked up by metal detectors or airport scanners.

THEO*ism* practitioners are concerned about the seamless interactivity between human and AI, and how that will impact on the essential characteristic of being human.

We are learning how the digital era is amplifying human effectiveness while threatening human independence.

The majority of humans are unaware of the fact that decisions are now being made for them by computers (AI).

We no longer have to think for ourselves because, smart systems in our vehicles, in buildings, on farms, and in business processes are saving us time and money.

Because AI cannot express empathy or emotion, traits native only to humans, AI is not a good match for areas such as social work, psychotherapy, or in-depth customer service.

AI is best suited for tasks such as algorithms that drive recommendation engines on platforms such as Amazon, Spotify, and Netflix.

Here is another example of how AI and humans team up for an entire production.

AI is faster in voice transcription than humans, but we cannot rely on AI alone to transcribe voice correctly when the speed, diction, accent, and tone of the speech vary, especially if there are background noises.

We need humans to verify transcription accuracy and to fix errors if required.

E-commerce, telemedicine, video streamings, internet radio, and coming soon, web-based TV are all programming humans to live online.

In and of itself, AI is not a technology to be feared.

What we should fear are individuals, businesses, and governments using AI to harm and for malicious purposes.

NAMASTE

www.ingramcontent.com/pod-product-compliance
Lightning Source LLC
Chambersburg PA
CBHW060544100426

42742CB00013B/2448